TIME ZONE

Jane Wood

Illustrated by Kate Rochester

OXFORD
UNIVERSITY PRESS

Contents

What's the Time? 4
Night or Day? 6
How Many Hours? 8
Today or Tomorrow? 10
Time to Eat 12
School Time 14
Playing and Relaxing 16
Time for Bed 18
A Day in Australia – Mia 20
A Day in Alaska, USA – Ethan 21
A Day in Hong Kong – Dennis 22
A Day in South Africa – Naledi 24
A Day in the UK – Michael 26
A Day in Brazil – Lucas 28
A Day in Wisconsin, USA – Brianna 29
Glossary 30
Index 31

What's the Time?

How often do you ask:

What time is it?

You could use a watch or a clock to find out. You could check on a mobile phone or the radio or television. They will all give you a similar answer.

But what if you were somewhere else? Someone asking the same question, at the same moment, but in another part of the world, could get a completely different answer!

Brianna

1 am Tuesday — 3 MARCH

Madison, Wisconsin, USA

Monday has finished. Tuesday began an hour ago here.

Ethan

10 pm Monday — 2 MARCH

Nome, Alaska, USA

It's bedtime on Monday night for me.

Lucas

4 am Tuesday — 3 MARCH

Rio de Janeiro, Brazil

Monday finished here four hours ago. It's very early in the morning.

Michael

7 am Tuesday 3 MARCH

London, UK

My alarm clock has just gone off. It's time to get up.

Dennis

3 pm Tuesday 3 MARCH

Hong Kong

My school day has finished. I'll be home soon.

Mia

5 pm Tuesday 3 MARCH

Queensland, Australia

It's nearly time to eat dinner.

Naledi

9 am Tuesday 3 MARCH

Limpopo, South Africa

My day at school has already started.

We'll catch up with these new friends again soon.

Night or Day?

Time to get up in London

Because the Earth is round, only half of it is lit by the Sun at a time. As the Earth rotates, different parts are lit.

Bedtime in Alaska

Middle of the night in Wisconsin

When the Earth is facing away from the Sun, it is dark. Here it is night.

Very early in Rio de Janeiro

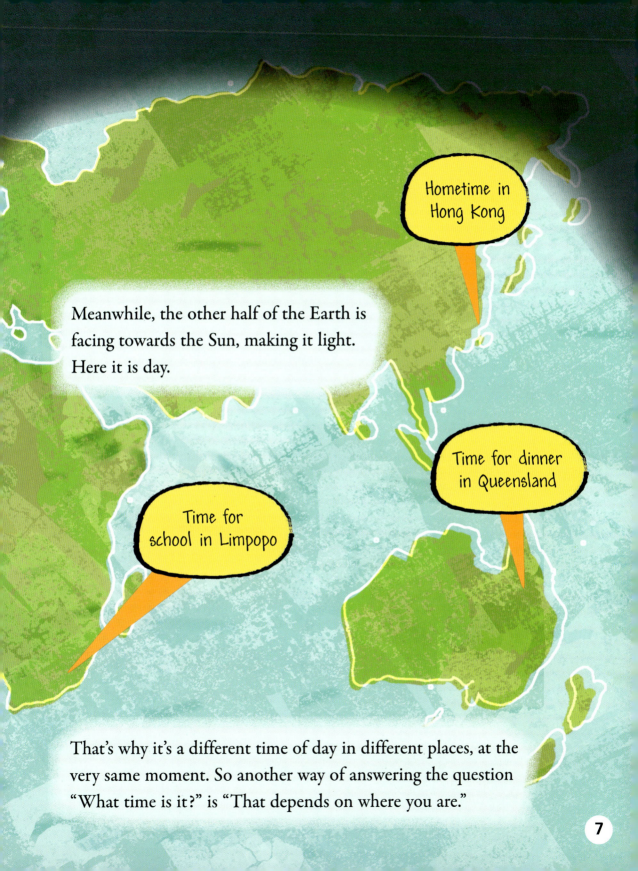

Hometime in Hong Kong

Meanwhile, the other half of the Earth is facing towards the Sun, making it light. Here it is day.

Time for dinner in Queensland

Time for school in Limpopo

That's why it's a different time of day in different places, at the very same moment. So another way of answering the question "What time is it?" is "That depends on where you are."

How Many Hours?

An imaginary line known as the Greenwich Meridian runs from the North Pole to the South Pole, straight through Greenwich (*say* gren-ich) in London. The time at Greenwich is known as Greenwich Mean Time, or GMT.

Because all of the labelled places are located along the Greenwich Meridian, it's 12 noon at the same time in all of them.

France

Algeria

Mali

Togo

In fact, imaginary lines known as meridians divide the whole world up into 24 time zones, one hour apart. Within each time zone it is the same time.

Antarctica

-11 -10 -9 -8 -7 -6 -5 -4 -3 -2 -1 0

Today or Tomorrow?

On the opposite side of the Earth to the Greenwich Meridian is another line called the International Date Line. This marks the place where the date first changes each day. The time zone to its west is the first place in the world to get the new day's date. The time zone to its east is the last place to get the same date, 24 hours later.

It's the start of Tuesday, 3rd March here.

It's the start of Monday, 2nd March here.

International Date Line

Equator

The International Date Line isn't visible on the surface of the planet. It's an imaginary line which is only drawn on maps, just like the **equator** and the Greenwich Meridian.

On the Greenwich Meridian, it's 12 noon on Monday, 2nd March.

FACT

People who have sailed across the equator are nicknamed 'shellbacks'. A 'golden shellback' is someone who has sailed over the point where the equator crosses the International Date Line!

Time to Eat

Let's find out more about how our friends around the world spend their days.

What kinds of food do they eat?

Brianna Wisconsin, USA: 4 am

It's four hours until breakfast time! I'll have a cinnamon roll, fruit and milk at my school breakfast club.

Ethan Alaska, USA: 1 am

When I get up in six hours' time I'll probably have reindeer sausage for breakfast. Sometimes I have wild blueberry muffins, pancakes or fish.

Lucas Rio de Janeiro, Brazil: 7 am

I like bread and chocolate milk for breakfast. Sometimes we have fruit like papaya.

Michael
London, UK: 10 am

It's nearly breaktime. Today I've brought an apple for my snack.

Dennis
Hong Kong: 6 pm

Grandma has made beef hotpot and fried rice for dinner. We'll have tangyuan afterwards – sweet rice dumplings filled with nuts.

Mia
Queensland, Australia: 8 pm

I have a glass of milk before I go to bed.

Naledi
Limpopo, South Africa: 12 noon

It's nearly lunchtime. We usually have **pap** with vegetable stew, or **samp** and beans, made from vegetables we've grown in the school garden.

School Time

What happens on school days?

Brianna
Wisconsin, USA: 6 pm

I stay at after-school club from 3 to 6 pm. School started at 8.45 am so it has been a long day.

Ethan
Alaska, USA: 3 pm

It's 30 minutes until hometime. After school, I'll go snowboarding with my friends while it's still light.

Lucas
Rio de Janeiro, Brazil: 9 pm

I'm just falling asleep, but I'm looking forward to the Carnival, when there's no school and we all go to bed very late!

Michael
London, UK: 12 midnight

I'll get up in about seven hours. My class starts the school day with 'wake and shake' exercises at 8.55 am.

Dennis
Hong Kong: 8 am

My school day will start soon. Today we'll study maths, Chinese, science, sports and music.

Maths : 8.40–9.35	Sports : 1.00–2.00
Chinese : 9.35–10.30	Music : 2.00–3.00
Science : 10.30–12.00	Hometime
Lunch	

Mia
Queensland, Australia: 10 am

I'm in my classroom at home, having a lesson on my computer. My teacher is 300 kilometres away!

Naledi
Limpopo, South Africa: 2 am

I'm asleep. I'll get up at 6 am. I'll walk three kilometres to school, ready to start lessons at 7.30 am.

Playing and Relaxing

What does everyone do for fun?

Ethan
Alaska, USA: 10 pm

It was too dark and cold to play outside for long this evening. Instead I watched the news. It was about the Iditarod, a 1600-kilometre sled dog race across Alaska that finishes in my home town, Nome.

Brianna
Wisconsin, USA: 1 am

I've been asleep for hours. I'm tired after playing outside with my friends.

Lucas
Rio de Janeiro, Brazil: 4 am

I'm asleep, probably dreaming about my favourite thing – playing football!

Michael
London, UK: 7 am

I feed my pets every morning. Sometimes I help to walk my dog before school, too.

Dennis
Hong Kong: 3 pm

Some days I stay for after-school activities. I like Chinese drumming and swimming best.

Mia
Queensland, Australia: 5 pm

I help to **muster** the cattle. It's really exciting, and I love riding my horse.

Naledi Limpopo, South Africa: 9 am

I feed the chickens before I leave home. At school I help to care for the garden.

Time for Bed

What happens at the end of the day?

Brianna
Wisconsin, USA: 12 noon
I'm at school – I won't be going to bed for hours!

Ethan
Alaska, USA: 9 am
The sun is only just coming up. In winter it doesn't rise all day. In summer it's sunny for 24 hours and I go to bed in the light!

Lucas
Rio de Janeiro, Brazil: 3 pm
I finished school at 1 pm. I have a **siesta** in the afternoon, and after that I go out to play.

Michael London, UK: 6 pm

6 pm – Dinner
7 pm – Cub Scouts
8.30 pm – Bath and bed. Read.

Dennis
Hong Kong: 2 am

It never gets dark at night here because of all the city lights.

Mia
Queensland, Australia: 4 am

There are no street lights here in the **outback**. It's so dark at night I can see thousands of stars.

Naledi Limpopo, South Africa: 8 pm

I go to bed about an hour after sunset, once it gets really dark.

A Day in Australia – Mia

Because I live a long way from the nearest school, I study with the School of the Air. My teacher is 300 kilometres away but I talk to him every day on my computer. Once a term, my teacher flies out to visit me.

I meet my friends once a year at school camp.

After lessons, I help on our cattle station or ride my horse or **quad bike**.

A Day in Alaska, USA – Ethan

THE IDITAROD

Every year in March, Ethan watches some of the Iditarod (*say* eye-dit-a-rod) in Alaska. This extreme sled dog race takes 10–14 days to complete. Teams of 16 dogs pull their **musher's** sled more than 1600 kilometres. They cross icy **tundra**, frozen rivers and snowy mountains. Some teams have to drop out. Prize money is given to the teams that actually complete the race.

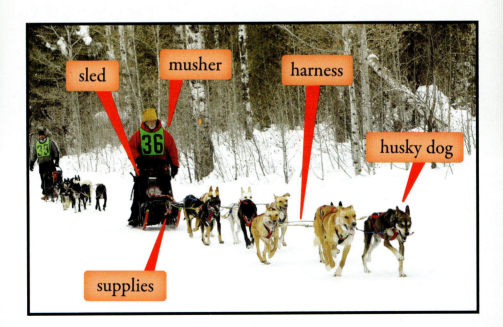

A Day in Hong Kong – Dennis

Dear Brianna,

Many children in Hong Kong study very hard. I have homework every day and extra English lessons at the weekend. In my free time, I like to watch TV, swim and play computer games. I also read manga comics and do **martial arts**.

At the weekend, friends come over to play or I go out with my family. I like going to Tai Yuen Street, which is famous for its toy shops.

Sometimes we visit mainland China or catch the ferry to Macau. Macau has some beautiful buildings and gardens. It also has the world's highest bungee jump!

Best wishes,

Dennis Wai Yi Lap

A Day in South Africa – Naledi

South Africa is a hot, dry country. Many people have to walk a long way to fetch water. My school gets water from its own well. We use it for drinking, cooking, washing, **sanitation** and to water the school garden. Everyone helps to look after the garden. We sow seeds, water plants, do weeding and pick **crops**. Then we eat what we've grown for our school lunches.

The school shares some of the **surplus** crops with orphans. The rest of the fruit and vegetables are sold, which makes money to pay for:

- school books
- equipment
- a clinic to keep us healthy.

cabbage

bell peppers

tomatoes

A Day in the UK – Michael

Monday – Michael's homework set
Lunchtime singing club

Tuesday – Outdoor sports: take PE kit

Wednesday – Bikeability training
(lunchtime, in school playground)

Thursday – Indoor games: take PE kit

Friday – Michael's homework due in

Michael needs these for Bikeability training:

helmet

high-vis jacket

What will you learn in Bikeability training?

1 How to control your bike

2 How and where you can cycle safely

3 Hazards to look out for

4 How to keep your bike in safe working order

EARN BADGES AS YOUR SKILLS AND CONFIDENCE IMPROVE!

A Day in Brazil – Lucas

My city is famous for the beaches, mountains and rainforests that surround it – and for the Carnival!

The Rio de Janeiro Carnival is held at the end of summer and is spread over five days. Thousands of people come to take part or to watch the parades. We spend a lot of time making our own costumes. We enjoy seeing the amazing costumes that other people have created, too.

A Day in Wisconsin, USA – Brianna

Hi Dennis,

Lots of parents work late, so me and my friends stay at after-school club until 6 pm. I do my homework, play games with my friends, or do arts and crafts. It is snowy in Wisconsin now. I like playing in the snow at after-school club, although I have to change into dry clothes afterwards!

Bye for now,

Brianna

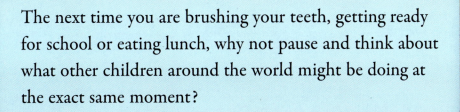

The next time you are brushing your teeth, getting ready for school or eating lunch, why not pause and think about what other children around the world might be doing at the exact same moment?

Glossary

crops: fruits, vegetables, beans and seeds that have been grown for food

equator: an imaginary line around the middle of the Earth

high-vis: short for 'high-visibility' – a brightly coloured, reflective item that allows someone to be seen easily

martial arts: sports like judo in which people practise self-defence or attack

musher: driver of a dog sled

muster: to gather farm animals, like cows or horses, together

outback: an area of Australia where few people live, which is a long way from the coast and cities

pap: thick porridge made from ground maize (corn)

quad bike: a motor cycle with four wheels, for travelling off-road

samp: dried corn made into a stew

sanitation: the process of making something clean

siesta: a short sleep in the middle of the day

surplus: extra or more than you need

tundra: the large area in the Arctic where it is too cold for trees to grow

Index

Alaska 4, 12, 14, 16, 18, 21
Australia 5, 9, 13, 15, 17, 19, 20
Brazil 4, 12, 14, 16, 18, 28
cycling 26–27
Earth 6–7, 10
food 12–13, 24–25
Greenwich Mean Time 8
Greenwich Meridian 8, 10–11
homework 22, 26, 29
Hong Kong 5, 13, 15, 17, 19, 22–23
Iditarod 16, 21
International Date Line 10–11
play 16, 18, 22, 23, 29
sleep 4, 14, 15, 16
South Africa 5, 13, 15, 17, 19, 24–25
sport 14, 15, 16, 21, 26
Sun 6–7, 18, 19
UK 5, 8, 13, 15, 17, 19, 26–27
USA 4, 12, 14, 16, 18, 21, 29

31

About the Author

When I was at school in England, I joined a penpal club. Soon I received letters from Canada, Haiti, France, Belgium, Luxembourg, the Netherlands, India, Japan and New Zealand.

I remember wondering what my penpals were doing while I was eating my breakfast. I discovered that things that were ordinary for me seemed strange and unusual to them, and vice-versa.

Some only wrote a few times. Most wrote for a few years. Just one remains in touch today. I thought about my penpals a lot whilst writing this book, so I'd like to dedicate it to Laura, Rosa, Fredericke, Nathalie, Josée, Irma, Tomoko and Ann-Marie, wherever they are now; and especially to Ruby, in India – a lifelong friend I've never met.

Greg Foot, Series Editor

I've loved science ever since the day I took my papier mâché volcano into school. I filled it with far too much baking powder, vinegar and red food colouring, and WHOOSH! I covered the classroom ceiling in red goo. Now I've got the best job in the world: I present TV shows for the BBC, answer kids' science questions on YouTube, and make huge explosions on stage at festivals!

Working on TreeTops inFact has been great fun. There are so many brilliant books, and guess what … they're all packed full of awesome facts! What's your favourite?